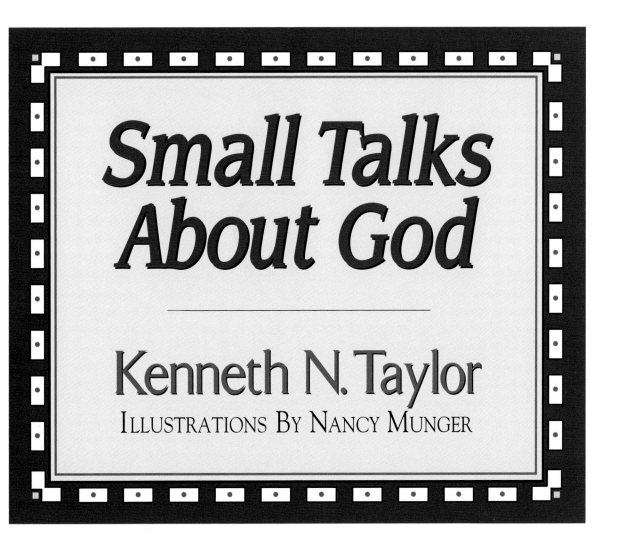

Small Talks About God

Kenneth N. Taylor

ILLUSTRATIONS BY NANCY MUNGER

MOODY PRESS
CHICAGO

Printed in the United States of America

CONTENTS

Heaven

o you know where heaven is? Heaven is a place somewhere far beyond the sky where Jesus and the angels live. It is a beautiful place, more beautiful than you have ever seen. Heaven is God's home, so everything there is bright and beautiful, and no one is ever sick or sad.

Would you like to go there some day and see such a wonderful place? Lots of other kids who are Jesus' friends are there, and they're very, very happy. Yes, I'm sure you would like to go there too, and I'll tell you how.

This little boy and girl in the picture want to go to heaven. They are looking up into the sky, trying to see the road that goes there. But soon they'll find out something nice, and I'll tell you what it is. They don't need a road or a street to get to heaven. Isn't that strange? There *is* no road to heaven, but someday Jesus will come and get us, if we want Him to, and take us there.

Everyone who loves Jesus can get to heaven that way. They can live there always in that beautiful place where everyone is happy and good.

A STORY

One day Josh and Amy were pretending to be explorers. They were looking for the road to heaven. They loved Jesus and wanted to see Him and be near Him because He loves children. That night they asked their father, "How can we get to heaven? We can't find the road that goes up into the sky."

Their father laughed with surprise and answered, "Sweethearts, you can't get to heaven by walking or riding. You have to wait until Jesus comes to get you, and then He will take us all up into the sky with Him."

"When will Jesus come to get us?" Amy wanted to know.

"Jesus hasn't told us that," Dad said, "so you run downstairs and help your mom with dinner. Because when you are kind and helpful Jesus is happy."

And that is just what they did.

? SOME QUESTIONS

1. What are the little boy and girl in the picture trying to find?
2. Is there a street that goes up into the sky?
3. How can people get to heaven?

A PRAYER

Dear Jesus, thank You for the nice home you're making for me up there in heaven. Help me to love You and do the things You want me to. Amen.

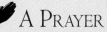 A BIBLE THOUGHT

Jesus said: I am going away to make a home for you in heaven, and then I will come back and get you so that you can live there with Me always.

John 14:2–3

BIBLE READING—JOHN 14: 1–6

The angels

Have you ever seen an angel? No, not very many people have, because when the angels walk around nobody can see them unless the angels want them to. Probably some of them are right here with us in this room, but we can't see or feel them. Wouldn't it be fun to be an angel?

But you see, God doesn't want you just to be an angel, even though that would be so much fun. God doesn't want you to be an angel, because He wants you to be His child. God wants you to be in His family. It is much better to be God's child than to be one of His angels.

What do the angels do? They are God's helpers, and they help God's children. They help you and me. One of their jobs is to keep us from getting hurt, like in this picture. Do you see the angel taking care of the little children? They can't see the angel, but the angel is keeping them from falling. If one of the children slips, maybe the angel will push him back again. That's what angels do sometimes.

Wherever God's children go, angels are there to help them. Let's thank God because we can be His children and have angels to help us.

A Story

This is a Bible story about the way God sent His angels to take care of two of His friends.

Elisha was the name of a good man who did whatever God told him to. Many people didn't like Elisha because God told him to tell the people they were bad. The people didn't like this, so they came to catch Elisha and hurt him.

Just then Elisha looked up and saw God's angels coming to help him. Elisha could see them, but no one else knew they were there. Even Elisha's friend who was standing there with him couldn't see them at first, so Elisha asked God to make his friend's eyes so that he could see the angels too. God did this, and then both of them saw the angels, and the angels helped them and took care of them.

? Some Questions

1. Are there any angels here in this room?
2. Can we always see the angels? Can they see us?
3. Who sends the angels to help us?

 A Prayer

Our Father in heaven, thank You for Your angels that You send to help us. We want to be Your helpers too. Thank You for being so kind to us. In Jesus' name we pray. Amen.

A Bible Thought

He sends His angels to be our helpers.
Hebrews 1:14

BIBLE READING—2 KINGS 6:8–17

You may talk with the King!

J ust imagine that you could go any time you wanted to and talk to a great king who would gladly give you anything you needed!

That would be very exciting and wonderful. But it would be ever so much more wonderful if you received an invitation from the great God of heaven to come and talk to Him. Do you know that God has invited you to come and talk with Him? He's even disappointed if you don't! He wants you to ask Him for things you need. He loves to give you things. He enjoys having you talk with Him.

Think of it! God, who is so holy and pure, is willing to talk to you. He will not think you are bothering Him. He loves you and wants you to come to Him.

Do you see what this girl in the picture is doing? She's talking to God! God in heaven is listening to her while she talks to Him. Would you like to talk to Him too?

You can talk to Him at night when you go to bed, and when you are walking to school, and when you get home, and at any other time. God is always glad to talk with you. Isn't that great?

A STORY

T his is a true story of something that happened long ago. Several children and their mothers were out walking one day. They saw Jesus talking to some men who were His friends. The children wanted to talk to Jesus because He was their friend too. Their mothers took them by the hand, and they all went to talk to Jesus.

But when the men saw them coming, they were angry. "Go away," they scolded. "Don't bother Jesus; He is too important to talk to kids. Mothers, take those children away."

I think the children cried, don't you? They just wanted to talk to Jesus, and the men wouldn't let them.

But then a great thing happened. Jesus saw that the men were sending the children away.

"Oh, don't do that," He said. "Let the little children come to Me. I want to talk to them." So the men stepped back and let them come. Jesus sat them on His lap and talked to them. They were so happy then!

Would you like to come and talk to Jesus?

He wants you to, and He won't let anyone shoo you away.

? SOME QUESTIONS

1. Where does Jesus live?
2. Can He hear you when you talk to Him?
3. Does Jesus like you to talk to Him?
4. Can you talk to Jesus even if you can't see Him?

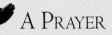 A PRAYER

Dear Jesus, thank You for letting us come and talk to You even though You are so great and we are so small. Please help me to love You and to come often to You just as we are doing now. Amen.

A BIBLE THOUGHT

Jesus said, Let the little children come to Me.

Matthew 19:14

BIBLE READING—LUKE 18:15–17

Who made everything?

This little girl is talking to the man on the tractor. A tractor is like a car, but it goes through fields on its big wheels and pulls heavy things after it. The man is using the tractor to pull a plow that breaks up the ground. Then he'll put seeds in the soft, warm soil, and soon green leaves of corn or wheat will grow.

The big tractor can help get the ground ready to put in the tiny seeds, but it can't make the seeds grow. Only God can do that. God can do it because He is so great. God makes seeds and flowers, and He made the rocks and the sky. He made the sun and the moon and all the stars. And God made you.

You and I cannot make stars. We can make little things with a saw or a hammer, but only God can make stars and things like that. God is so great that He can do whatever He wants to, no matter what.

And always, always remember this: God loves you very, very much. You are one of His dear children. He loves you and gave Himself to die for you.

A Story

Nathan and Jennifer were excited about something. They had been outside playing, and they saw a pretty red flower.

"Oh, look," Jennifer said, "what a pretty flower! I wish there were two flowers instead of one."

"Well, let's make another," Nathan said. "Then we'll have two."

"You can't make flowers," Jennifer told him. "They just have to grow. You put a seed in the ground, and it grows up and becomes a pretty flower."

"Well, then, let's make a seed," Nathan said.

They ran into the house and got flour from Mom and put just a little water with it until they could form little white balls by rolling it between their fingers.

"See our seeds," they said to Mom. "Aren't they pretty?"

Then they colored them red and blue with their paint set and took them outside and put them in the soft ground.

"Now we'll have a red flower and a blue flower," Nathan said. "Pretty soon our seeds will grow, and we will have some pretty flowers."

But Jennifer didn't think so.

Who do you think was right?

? Some Questions

1. Can people make seeds that will grow?
2. Who can?
3. Who can make stars?
4. Who made you?

A Prayer

O God, our heavenly Father, thank You for being so great and so good. Thank You for making me and for loving me. Please help me to love You and to do the things You'd like me to. In Jesus' name. Amen.

 A Bible Thought

All things were made by Him.

John 1:3

BIBLE READING—GENESIS 1:1–8

Jesus loves you

These kids are looking at a picture and singing a song. Do you know who they're looking at in the picture? Yes, it is a picture of Jesus with some children. Jesus loves children and their dads and moms too. He wants them to come to Him so He can help them and talk to them. I'll tell you what song the children are singing as they look at the picture. They are singing,

Jesus loves me this I know.
For the Bible tells me so.
Little ones to Him belong,
They are weak, but He is strong.

Yes, Jesus loves me,
Yes, Jesus loves me,
Yes, Jesus loves me,
The Bible tells me so.

Do you know that Jesus loves you just as He loves the children in the picture? He wants to talk to you and help you. He wants to be your friend always and always and always. No one but Jesus can take you up to heaven when you die. Only Jesus' friends can be in heaven with Him, because that is what God says. Are you a friend of Jesus? Will you do whatever He tells you to? Can you decide right now that whatever Jesus tells you, you will do? Then you will be Jesus' friend, and He will be your friend forever.

A Story

Kaitlyn was crying. Mom told her to put her dolls away, and she said, "No," and so her mother had given her time-out for not doing what she was told. That night after dinner when Mother had kissed her and tucked her into bed, Kaitlyn started crying again.

"Why, Kaitlyn, Mom called, what's the matter?"

"I'm sorry I said I wouldn't put my dolls away," Kaitlyn sobbed, "and now Jesus doesn't like me anymore."

"Oh," her mother said, "so that's it." And then she told Kaitlyn some great news. "Jesus still loves you just as much," she said. "Jesus died on the cross because of what you did. He knew you were going to disobey this afternoon, and He died for you so that God could forgive you. He took away the badness. That's how much He loves you. Let's thank Him for taking God's punishment for what you did."

So Kaitlyn and her mother bowed their heads and thanked God for Jesus and His love.

? Some Questions

1. What did Kaitlyn do that was bad?
2. Did God punish Kaitlyn for disobeying?
3. Whom did God punish instead?

A Prayer

Father above, thank You so much for Jesus. And thank You, Jesus, for coming down from heaven and dying for me. Amen.

A Bible Thought

God loves you so much that He punished Jesus for the bad things you do.

John 3:16

BIBLE READING—ISAIAH 53:4–6

Don't fight!

It's very easy to make people angry. All you have to do is say, "You did too," if they say they didn't. Or you can call them names, and then they'll probably call you something you don't like, and then there will be a big fight. Or you can tease your little brother and sister and play with their toys and other things when they don't want you to. You can almost always make them mad by doing this.

But that is not the way a Christian should act. Should a Christian try to make people angry and upset? No, of course not. A Christian should try to make people happy instead of angry. It's easy to make people cry, but God wants us to help them feel happy.

The girl in this picture is whispering in her brother's ear. She's telling him a secret. She's saying that the kids who live across the street are nice. Now this girl and her brother will go over and play and have lots of fun with their neighbors.

Jesus likes us to say good things about other people whenever we can, because then people will know that we are friends of His. People will think, "Well, if Jesus' friends are nice, then Jesus must be best of all."

A Story

Once there was a man named Isaac. Isaac had many sheep. It was a hot day, and the sheep were thirsty. They wanted to drink some water, but there wasn't any, so Isaac and his friends dug a deep hole in the ground called a well. They found water down in the bottom of the hole and tied a bucket to a rope to get the water out, so the sheep could drink.

But some men came along and said to Isaac's friends, "Go away. This is our water."

"No," said Isaac's men, "we dug this well, and it is ours."

The men were going to hit each other and fight about it. Then Isaac said, "No, don't fight. Let those men have the well, and we'll go away and dig another one." So that's what they did. Isaac and his friends and his sheep went away. They wouldn't argue and fight, because they knew God didn't want them to. This is a true story. It's in the Bible.

? Some Questions

1. Did Isaac let his men fight about the well?
2. Should a friend of Jesus try to make other people cry?
3. Can you think of some way to make another child happy? How would you do it?

A Prayer

Dear Father in heaven, please help me to be kind to other people, and to help them and not fight with them or make them angry. And thank You for helping Isaac. Amen.

A Bible Thought

It is good to make peace.

Matthew 5:9

BIBLE READING—GENESIS 26:17–22

Helping things that are hurt

his little girl is being kind to her kitten. It was hungry. The kitten saw the little girl eating her breakfast, so it was mewing. Now the little girl is feeding it.

Aren't you glad the girl is being kind to the kitten? God likes this too. He says in the Bible that He will give good things to people who are kind. You see, God up in heaven is watching everything that happens down here on earth. He knows all the birds and the animals, every one of them. He knows whenever one of them is sick or hurt. He knows when the kittens are hungry; and God knows whenever a child is kind to one of these birds or animals that He has made. God is happy when kids are kind. When we are kind, that shows that we are trying to do what God wants.

We can be kind to people too, not just to kittens or birds. Can you think of someone you can be kind to? What could you do for him or her that would be nice, and kind?

A Story

There is a story in the Bible about a man who was going on a trip. He was walking along the road when some robbers jumped on him and took away all his money and knocked him down and hurt him. Then they ran away. The man couldn't get up because he was so badly hurt. Then another man came along, and the man who was hurt was very happy because now someone could help him. But the man didn't stop. He looked at the hurt man but walked on without helping him at all. Another man passed by, but he did not stop either.

Then a third man came along, and he stopped and helped the man who was lying there. He put bandages and medicine on his hurts. He was kind to the man who was hurt. God liked this. Jesus told the people about this good man and said we should help people too.

? Some Questions

1. Was the good man kind? What did he do?
2. Does God like us to be kind?
3. Have you ever been kind by helping something or someone who was hurt or sick?

A Prayer

Dear God, we are often selfish. We are kind to ourselves instead of to other people. Please help us to be kind to others and try to help them so that You will be happy. Amen.

A Bible Thought

God says, Blessed are those who are kind; I will be kind to them too.

Matthew 5:7

BIBLE READING—LUKE 10:30–37

Pure in heart

This is a picture of a little girl who loves Jesus very much. She tries to do whatever He wants. One thing God wants her to do is always to obey her father and mother, and she tries to do this.

Another thing God wants her to do is to talk to Him, so she prays every night before she goes to sleep, and sometimes she prays during the day too. She can pray while she is playing and thank God for many things. She likes to think about Jesus while she is playing. Sometimes she stops and thinks about God's love, and it makes her very happy.

God loves this little girl. She thinks about God, and that pleases Him.

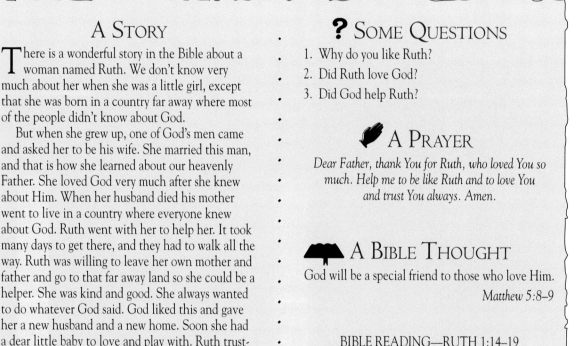

A Story

There is a wonderful story in the Bible about a woman named Ruth. We don't know very much about her when she was a little girl, except that she was born in a country far away where most of the people didn't know about God.

But when she grew up, one of God's men came and asked her to be his wife. She married this man, and that is how she learned about our heavenly Father. She loved God very much after she knew about Him. When her husband died his mother went to live in a country where everyone knew about God. Ruth went with her to help her. It took many days to get there, and they had to walk all the way. Ruth was willing to leave her own mother and father and go to that far away land so she could be a helper. She was kind and good. She always wanted to do whatever God said. God liked this and gave her a new husband and a new home. Soon she had a dear little baby to love and play with. Ruth trusted God, so God made her very happy.

? Some Questions

1. Why do you like Ruth?
2. Did Ruth love God?
3. Did God help Ruth?

A Prayer

Dear Father, thank You for Ruth, who loved You so much. Help me to be like Ruth and to love You and trust You always. Amen.

A Bible Thought

God will be a special friend to those who love Him.

Matthew 5:8–9

BIBLE READING—RUTH 1:14–19

Being punished

Being punished isn't fun! No, it isn't fun at all! We don't like to get time-out or a spanking, and it makes us feel bad when we are scolded.

Should children be punished when they do wrong things, or would it be better to just let them go ahead and be bad? What would happen if children were never punished?

Those children would become worse and worse. If they did something wrong and weren't punished for it, they would do that wrong thing again and again. Soon they would decide to do something even worse. Since nobody punished them, they would never try to stop doing wrong.

It is much better to be punished when we do wrong things so that we will remember not to do them again!

Why do we do bad things? It is because we have sin in our hearts. Satan keeps trying to get us to do things that God says we must not do.

And when we have done wrong, what should we do about it? We must tell Jesus we are sorry and ask Him to forgive us. And we should also tell Mother or Father that we are sorry.

A Story

Heather was hiding behind the sofa. She didn't want to help her mom wash the dishes, so she was hiding.

"Heather," her mother called, "please come right away and help me with the dishes.

But Heather just stayed where she was and didn't say anything.

"Heather," her mother called again. Then she came in to see why Heather didn't come. "Heather," her mother said, "I think you are behind the sofa. Please come out right now, or I'll have to punish you. Come now, or you can't have cookies this afternoon."

Heather did not come.

But after a while Heather got tired of staying behind the sofa. She came out and helped Mom do the dishes. Afterward she said, "Mom, I helped with the dishes, now may I have some cookies?"

"No," Mom said, "not today. You know what I told you. No cookies today because you didn't come when I asked you to."

Heather cried and cried, but she didn't get any cookies. And the next day when her mother called her to help with the dishes she didn't want to miss any cookies. So can you guess what she did when she heard her mother calling? She came right away!

I would too, wouldn't you?

? Some Questions

1. Why was Heather hiding?
2. What happened because she didn't come?
3. Do you think Heather comes now when her mother calls her?

A Prayer

Dear Father in heaven, You know when I've been bad and I am sorry that I've done things I shouldn't. Thank You for Jesus, who died for my sins. Thank You for Mom and Dad who help me to be good. Amen.

A Bible Thought

Children, obey your fathers and mothers.

Ephesians 6:1

BIBLE READING—HEBREWS 12:5–11

There is only one God

id you ever have a puppy to play with? Was it warm and soft and wiggly?

Sometimes puppies get lost. Somebody comes walking along and the puppy follows him, and then what will happen? Pretty soon the puppy wants to come home again, but he doesn't know where home is, so you have to go and find him, and you say, "Now puppy, stay home. Don't follow other people. You stay home with me, because I don't want you to get lost."

God loves you more than you love your puppy, so God says, "Don't run away from Me. Don't pray to anyone else." There is only one God, and if anyone says there are others, you must not believe it. Only our God can hear us when we pray. Only He will love us every day.

In this picture you can see some people who have made a god with their hammers and nails, and now they are going to kneel down and pray to it. What a strange thing to do! That is not a god; it is just something they made, and yet they think it can hear them and do things for them.

God does not like this. God does not want people to pray to foolish things but only to Him.

A Story

Ro is a little boy who lives in another country far away. One day Ro's daddy said to him, "Come, we must go and buy ourselves a god so that we can pray to him."

"OK, Daddy," Ro said. "I will go with you."

Ro and his father went to the store. It was a store that sold many kinds of little idols like the one in the picture. Some of them were pretty, and some of them were very ugly. Some of them had several arms and several heads. Ro's father bought one that had lots of arms. They took it home and put it on a shelf in their house.

"Now," said Ro's father, "let's call the rest of the family, and we will bow down and worship our new god. Perhaps he will give us food and help us."

So that is what Ro's family did. Do you think this was good?

❓ Some Questions

1. Where is God?
2. Can God hear us when we talk to Him? Can an idol hear us?
3. Can God see whatever we do? Can an idol see us?
4. Does God like it when people pray to an idol?

A Prayer

Thank You, O God, our heavenly Father, that we can pray to you and that You like us to come and talk to You. Help us never to pray to anyone else, and help people like Ro and his family to hear about You so that they won't worship an idol anymore. In Jesus' name. Amen.

 A Bible Thought

We must love God very, very much.
Matthew 22:37–38

BIBLE READING—JEREMIAH 10:3–5

Saying thank you to God

I n this picture you can see a little boy praying. He is saying thank you to God. He is thanking God for

Loving him, and for

Sending Jesus to die for his sins,

and for His father and mother,

and for a warm house,

and for enough food.

Can you think of other things he can be thankful for? Something else is a school where he can learn to read and write and use a computer.

We must love god more than anyone else. We should love Him even more than we love our fathers and mothers and our friends. This pleases Him and makes us happy too.

A STORY

B lossom is the name of a child far away in another country. She was playing in the street one day when a friend came running up to her. Her friend said, "Blossom, I have just heard something very nice. I want to tell you what I heard. I heard about a man named Jesus. He is God's Son and lives in heaven. He loves us and wants us to love Him. He died for our sins."

Blossom was very glad to hear this good news. No one had ever told her this before. She went with her friend to a place where other boys and girls were listening to a lady tell about Jesus. Blossom was very happy. She went home and told her father and mother about Jesus. They were happy to know about him too. Now Blossom's whole family loves God, and thanks Him every day for all He has done for them. She has a brother and a sister, and they love Jesus, too. Aren't you glad that Blossom's friend told her about Jesus?

? SOME QUESTIONS

1. What did Blossom's friend tell her?
2. Do you love God?
3. Have you told Him so?
4. Do you have a friend who needs to know about Jesus?

A PRAYER

Dear Father, thank You for being our only true God, who hears us up in heaven when we pray. Thank you for loving me, and dying for my sins. Amen.

A BIBLE THOUGHT

You must love the Lord your God.

Luke 10:27

BIBLE READING—JOHN 15:9–14

No swearing

"**Y**ou're bad," Jamie told his friend Brett. "I don't like you. I hope God hates you."

But Jamie didn't mean that at all. He was just talking and was angry at Brett. That's why he said that he wanted God to hate Brett.

But Jamie was saying something that makes God angry. Jamie was playing with God's great, wonderful name just as though it was a name like yours and mine. But God's name is different. The Bible tells us that His name is so great that some day when God's name is said, everybody will fall down. They will do this because they will have so much respect for God and His name. So you see, God's name is not something to say when we are angry.

But if we love God, then we can call Him by His wonderful name when we pray, and He will listen to us and help us. We should thank God every day for telling us His name so that we can talk to Him.

So now do you see why Jamie should never, never say God's name except in ways God likes? Yes, we must be very careful about this, because we want to please God and make Him happy.

What should we do if we have made God unhappy by saying His name in ways we shouldn't? He is very kind to those who tell Him they are sorry. He can forgive us because Jesus died for our sins. How kind God is!

A STORY

Some children were talking about God. Stacy said, "I love God the very best of all." Jonathan said, "I love Jesus best." Holly who was listening to them said, "I love the Lord." Then Jonathan said, "But Jesus is God, isn't He? I think Jesus and God and the Lord are different names God has."

Then Michael said, "I think that is right. Which one of His names do you like best?"

And Holly said, "They are all God's names, and I like all of them best!"

❓ SOME QUESTIONS

1. Is it right for people to say God's name when they are angry at each other?

2. What are some of God's names?

3. Which of His names do you like best?

🙏 A PRAYER

Dear God, our Father in heaven, we are so glad that You are God and that Your name is so very great. Help us to be careful to say Your name in good ways and never in bad ways. We ask this in Jesus' wonderful name. Amen.

📖 A BIBLE THOUGHT

You must not say God's name in bad ways.

Exodus 20:7

BIBLE READING—DANIEL 2:19–23

Sunday is different

Have you ever had a birthday? Yes, of course you have. Did you have a party on your birthday, and did you get presents?

Yes, birthdays are very special days that we all love.

Did you know that all of us have another special day too? It is a special day that comes every week. Every Sunday is a special day to remember what God has done for us.

After God made the world and the stars, and the trees, and the grass, and everything else, He made a special day to rest. God rested and says that we should rest one day every week, and not work as we do on other days. We call our rest day *Sunday* or the *Lord's Day*. It is God's special day that He has given us.

On Sunday you can go to church and learn more about Jesus. And on Sunday afternoon perhaps Mom or Dad can read good books to you, or you can go for a walk with them. Sunday is special. It is the day our Lord Jesus became alive again after He had died for our sins.

When we rest on Sunday we can do better work for God on the other days of the week. Sunday is not a day just to have fun. It is a day when we can be quieter than usual and learn more about our heavenly Father.

A STORY

Mr. Grubbs came over to see Susan's father. Susan heard them talking about going away to a lake where they could have fun trying to catch some fish.

Mr. Grubbs said, "Boy, will we have fun! I hear the fish are really big there this year. Let's go over next Sunday and see how many we can catch."

Susan liked to eat fish. She thought of eating the fish her daddy would catch! She could almost taste how good they would be after Mom had cooked them.

But Susan was glad when her father said, "No, not on Sunday. We go to Sunday school and church on Sunday. Let's go on Saturday afternoon instead."

So that is what they did. They didn't go on the Lord's Day, but they went on Saturday. Susan got to go with them, and she caught a fish too!

? SOME QUESTIONS

1. What special day comes every week?
2. What are some special things to do on Sundays?

A PRAYER

Our Father in heaven, thank You for giving us Sunday as Your special day. Thank You that it is different from other days, and that we can rest from all our work and be glad, and that You are glad too. Amen.

 A BIBLE THOUGHT

Don't forget God's special day that comes every week.
Exodus 20:8

BIBLE READING—EXODUS 20:8

Doing what Mom and Dad say

Do you see how happy these children are? They're having fun. Mom told them to rake up the leaves that had fallen on the grass in the yard. Are they crying because their mother asked them to help her? No, they're laughing. They want to help their mom and dad and do whatever they say. They're being good and making God happy. God likes them to do whatever their mother or father ask them to. God is happy, and their mother and father are happy, and the children are happy too. So everybody is happy because they are doing what their mother told them to.

God wants us to love our mothers and fathers and help them. He likes us to wash the dishes and pick up our toys and put them away.

When you get bigger, God wants you to take care of your mother and father. They can take care of you now when you are small, but some day when you are all grown up, you will need to help them even more than you do now. And do you know something nice? God says He will do something wonderful for children who take care of their mother and father.

A STORY

Andrea's big brother Matt was talking to Mom and Dad.

"But Dad," he said, "you ought to sell our old car. It's too old. Everybody else has a new car, and we should too."

"No," said Dad, "we don't need one. Ours works fine. We'll keep it for a while."

When Dad had gone out, Matt began to act angry. He told Andrea they needed a new car. "I guess Dad doesn't love us," Matt told his little sister, "because he doesn't get a new car that we can ride around in."

Matt's little sister didn't like what he was saying. "You shouldn't say things like that about Daddy," Andrea said. Then she thought of a Bible verse she had learned in Sunday school. It said that children should listen to what their parents say, and respect them. Andrea said the verse to Matt. But he looked surprised and didn't say anything for awhile.

Later he went out to see his dad. "I'm going to wash the car, Dad," he said. "It's a good car, and we want to keep it looking nice."

So you can see that Andrea's Bible verse helped big brother Matt.

? SOME QUESTIONS

1. How loud should you cry when Mom asks you to help her?
2. Why are the children in the picture happy?
3. Is God glad when His children help other people?
4. What can you do now to help your mother or father? Ask them for some ideas.

A PRAYER

O most holy God in heaven, help me always to make You glad by obeying my father and my mother, just as our Lord Jesus honored His mother. This I ask in Jesus' name. Amen.

A BIBLE THOUGHT

Honor your father and mother, and I will give you a long, good life.

Exodus 20:12

BIBLE READING—EPHESIANS 6:1–4

Life is precious

ometimes cats catch baby birds or mice. The cats kill the little birds, and we don't like them to do this.

God tells us in the Bible not to kill. Does this mean not to kill mice? No, it isn't talking about mice or birds. God will let us kill them, if we need to. But He says never to hurt other people or make them die. We must never kill anyone.

Sometimes children like to play games where they just pretend they're shooting other people and killing them. I wonder if God likes this? Do you think God wants us to play as if we don't care about what He says is wrong?

Another thing God tells us is that we should like people and not want to hurt them. He wants us to love them. That is one way for us to make God happy.

A STORY

A boy named Scott was talking to his sister. They were talking about the girl who lived across the street. Her name is Tracy.

"I don't like Tracy at all," Scott's sister said. "She always breaks my dolls. I hate her!"

"Then you are worse than she is," Scott said. "It's not good to be mad at Tracy, even if she does break your dolls."

"It isn't either," Scott's sister said. "If people hurt you, then you should hurt them."

"Oh, no!" Scott told his sister. "It isn't that way at all! We're supposed to be nice to everybody and try to help them, even if they hurt us."

"Even if they break our dolls?" Scott's sister asked.

"Yes," Scott said, "because that's what Jesus says."

And Scott was right. Jesus wants us always to be kind to other people and not be angry with them and not want to hurt them.

? SOME QUESTIONS

1. Why was Scott's sister angry at Tracy?
2. Does God say to hurt people if they hurt us first?
3. What did Scott tell his sister?

A PRAYER

Lord Jesus, please help us to love people. Thank You for loving us even when we are bad. Help us to love other people even if they are bad. And help them to love You. We ask this in Your name. Amen.

A BIBLE THOUGHT

Be nice to people who try to hurt you, and don't try to get even with them.

Matthew 5:44

BIBLE READING—MATTHEW 5:44-48

Boys and girls

If you see a child walking along the street ahead of you, can you tell whether it is a boy or girl? It's usually easy, isn't it? Girls just look different than boys, even if they are wearing the same kinds of clothes.

And their bodies are made differently. Boys are usually stronger. They are made that way so they can protect their mothers and sisters. Girls aren't as strong as boys, because God made their bodies in such a wonderful way that some day they can be mothers and have babies. Boys aren't made that way. Boys can never be mothers. But some day when they grow up, boys can find the person God wants them to marry and then they can be fathers.

God has given us rules about how boys and girls should act when they are together.

They need to know that God says, "You must not commit adultery." This means that people who are married should love the person God has given them to be their husband or wife and should not love anyone else in the same way. It also means that the Lord Jesus wants both boys and girls to be strong and pure. They must not think wrong thoughts. Kissing and hugging each other before it is God's time often results in wrong thoughts that lead to doing wrong things. So decide now that you will not do anything that makes God sad.

A Story

"Stop that!" yelled Jeremy as he ran across the yard. "You leave Julie alone!" Jeremy ran over to where Mark and Julie were.

"Aw, I'm not hurting her," Mark said. Then he pushed Julie again and almost made her fall down. Julie was crying.

"Quit doing that right now!" Jeremy said as he ran up to them, all out of breath.

"You think you can make me stop?" Mark asked. "I guess I can push her if I want to. She's my sister."

"Oh, no, you can't," said Jeremy. "Not when I'm around."

Jeremy grabbed him and pushed him away. Julie helped, and pretty soon Mark decided to run away. He went around the house and hid behind a bush. While Mark was hiding, he thought about what Jeremy had said. He said that God didn't want him to act that way.

"I guess Jeremy is right," Mark said to himself. "I guess I won't do that any more." After that Mark tried to help Julie instead of hurting her.

? Some Questions

1. Should boys try to help girls?
2. What did Jeremy tell Mark to stop doing?
3. What did Mark decide?

A Prayer

Dear Father, thank You for sisters and brothers, and thank You for making both girls and boys. Right now be with the child I will marry some day. Amen.

A Bible Thought

People who are married must not want to marry someone else.

Matthew 5:31–32

BIBLE READING—GENESIS 24:62–67

Don't take it

These boys in the picture are taking candy that doesn't belong to them. They are stealing candy bars. These are big boys, and they should know it is wrong to steal. Even little children know that stealing is wrong. God tells us in the Bible, "Don't ever take anything that doesn't belong to you."

Why does God say this? Well, would you like someone to sneak away with one of your toys and then say it is his? No, you wouldn't like that at all. God doesn't like it either. And He knows what is right and wrong.

Have you ever stolen anything? If you have, do you know what to do? You should take back what you have stolen and give it to the person it belongs to. And then you should tell your mother or father, and they will help you tell God about it and ask Him to forgive you.

A Story

Michelle looked at the big doll sitting there on the chair. Michelle wished and wished she had such a big doll. But it wasn't hers. She was playing at Laura's house, and the big doll belonged to Laura.

Michelle wanted the doll so much that she decided to steal it. When no one was looking, she ran out of the house with it and took it home with her, just as fast as she could go. She came into her own house with the big doll in her arms and hid it behind the sofa where she had some other important things. Then she got a cookie and sat down to eat it and think about her new big doll.

"It's mine now," she said to herself. "I'm going to play with the big doll every single day all the rest of my life!"

But Michelle didn't really feel very happy. The more she thought about it, the worse she felt. *God doesn't like this,* she thought. *I'd better take the doll back to Laura.*

So she did.

Laura said, "Oh, were you playing outside with my big doll? That's nice. Let's play some more with her in here."

That night when Michelle was going to bed, she felt very happy. "Thank You, Lord," she said, "for helping me to take the big doll back."

? Some Questions

1. Who did the big doll belong to?
2. Who stole the doll?
3. What finally happened to the doll?
4. Is Michelle glad or sorry that she took the doll back to its own house?

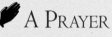 A Prayer

Dear Lord Jesus, help me always to love You and do what is right. Help me not to steal anything ever, even if I want it very much. And if I have stolen something, help me to take it back. Thank You for helping me. Amen.

A Bible Thought

If you have stolen something, take it back and never do it again.

Ephesians 4:28

BIBLE READING—LEVITICUS 19:11–13

Telling the truth

The boy in the picture is telling his friend about the fish he caught. He is showing how big it was. He says that it was so big that he could hardly lift it. I wonder if this boy is telling the truth. I think maybe he is telling a lie and trying to get the other boy to think that the fish was big when really it wasn't that big at all. What do you think about this? Is it all right to tell lies? No, God hates lies. He loves for us to tell the truth.

It is easy for us to say things that aren't true, but God says never do this. He wants us always to tell things right. If you do something wrong and somebody asks you if you did it, you should say yes. You might be punished, but you will be pleasing God. That is more important than anything else.

The Lord Jesus is true and pure. He tells no lies. God is pleased when His children say things that are right. Do you make God happy because you tell the truth?

A STORY

Eric and Gordon were brothers. These two brothers just loved to eat chocolate ice cream. Sometimes their mother let them have some in the afternoons, and sometimes she said no. One afternoon when Eric and Gordon had been playing outside a long time, they came into the kitchen as hungry as bears.

"Mom, may we have some chocolate ice cream?" they asked.

"Not this time," their mother said, "because it's almost dinner time."

But when she went upstairs to check on their baby sister, the boys quickly got out the chocolate ice cream and ate some. When they heard their mother coming downstairs, they quickly ate their last bite and started to play with some toys. Mom took one look at Eric's face. There was chocolate ice cream on it.

"Did you boys take some ice cream when I told you not to?" she asked.

"No," said Eric, "we didn't." But Eric forgot about the chocolate on his mouth! So Mother sent him to his room.

Gordon looked in the mirror. He didn't have any chocolate on his face.

"Did you take some too?" Mother asked him.

Gordon thought about what to say. If he told the truth, he knew what Mom would do. If he told a lie, he knew God wouldn't like that. Can you guess what he finally said?

? SOME QUESTIONS

1. Who always knows whether we are telling the truth or not?
2. How did Eric's mother know he was telling a lie?
3. Is it all right to tell little lies?

A PRAYER

Father in heaven, help me always to tell the truth even when I have done something wrong. May everyone know that I belong to You. Amen.

A BIBLE THOUGHT

Never tell lies.
Exodus 20:16

BIBLE READING—PHILIPPIANS 4:8–9

Wanting what belongs to other kids

his girl in the picture wishes she could catch a fish as her brother did. Do you see his fish? The girl doesn't have one yet and she feels bad. I think maybe she's going to cry.

But will it help her catch fish if she begins to cry? No, of course not. And do you know that God doesn't want her to cry about it or feel bad? God wants her to be happy that her brother has caught a nice fish instead of being sorry. God tells us in the Bible that it's not right to want other people's things.

Why is it wrong to want another child's toys? Because then you are really mad at God for not giving the toys to you. God knows what is best for you. If He doesn't want you to have a toy like another child's, then you should be happy without it and play with something else. God is always good, and God knows best. That is why we should be happy with whatever He gives us, and thank Him, and not want a lot of other things instead.

A Story

I want to tell you about a little boy called Gimmie! That wasn't his real name though. His real name was Jimmy , but people called him Gimmie because he always wanted other people's things. He kept saying, "Hey, gimmie this," or, "Hey, gimmie that!"

One day Gimmie's father gave him a bike. He took it outside to ride. While riding down the sidewalk he saw his friend Alan playing with a hammer.

So Gimmie cried and cried until his father came out to see what the trouble was.

"Alan won't give me his hammer," Gimmie said.

"But you have your bike," Father said. "Why don't you play with it?"

"I don't want a bike. I want a hammer!" Gimmie said.

"Gimmie that hammer," Gimmie said, but Alan wouldn't. So Gimmie's father took away the bike and gave him a hammer. Pretty soon Gimmie was crying again.

"I don't want this old hammer," he said. "Gimmie a truck. That's what I want."

Poor Gimmie. He had never learned to be happy with the things he had.

? Some Questions

1. Why was Jimmy called Gimmie?
2. Did he want a bike or a hammer or a truck?
3. Does Jesus want us to be happy with the things He gives us?

A Prayer

O Lord Jesus, help me to be glad and not complain. Help me know how great and kind You are, and help me not to want what belongs to other people. This I ask in Your name. Amen.

A Bible Thought

Be happy with what you have.
Hebrews 13:5

BIBLE READING—PSALM 23:1–6

Going to Sunday school

o you see what is happening in this picture? Two boys are going to Sunday school. Can you see the church waiting for them to come in? But now I will tell you a secret that the picture won't tell. The secret is that one of these boys has never been to Sunday school in his whole life. His mother and father don't know Jesus, so they never take him to Sunday school. But yesterday his friend asked him to come with him, and now they are almost there. Do you think he is going to have a good time at Sunday school learning about Jesus?

A STORY

"This is it," Daddy said as he stopped the car.

Stephanie looked at the big new house. It was the new house that Daddy had bought, and today was the day to begin living in it. Stephanie ran all around the house and liked everything she saw. Then she ran all through the house and stopped in every room.

"I like this house, Daddy," she said when she came back.

That afternoon, the little girl from next door came over to play. Her name was Kimberly.

"Can you go with me to Sunday school tomorrow?" Kimberly asked.

"Oh, I'd like to," Stephanie said, "but I've never been to Sunday school. Let's go and ask my mother."

Her mother said she could, so that is how Stephanie got a new house and a new friend and a new Sunday school, all at the same time.

? SOME QUESTIONS

1. Do you think God is glad because the girl next door asked Stephanie to come to Sunday school with her?
2. Do you know anyone who doesn't go to Sunday school?
3. Would you like to ask him (or her) to come with you next Sunday?

A PRAYER

Dear Father in heaven, there are so many children who never go to Sunday school and don't know about You. Please help me to invite other children to come and hear about Your love for them. Amen.

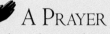 A BIBLE THOUGHT

Jesus said: Please go and tell other people how much I love them.

Mark 16:15

BIBLE READING—LUKE 6:6–11

Who should go to church?

Some people think that Sunday school is for children and church is just for mothers and fathers and older people. But that isn't true. Sunday school is for the whole family, and so is church.

Why is it so important to go to church? One reason is that God has commanded it, and that is really all the reason we need. Another reason is that it reminds us about how good and great God is. When we read the Bible and pray by ourselves, that is good. But when we see others worshiping God, that helps us to worship and praise Him even more than before.

When we're in church, we must be careful to be quiet and listen to what the pastor is saying. If there is a choir in our church, let's try to understand the words they are singing. When there is prayer, let's listen and say in our hearts the same words being said by the one praying out loud. During the sermon when the pastor is telling about what the Bible says, let's listen and not think about other things. Let's think about what is being said. We might not understand it all, but if we listen we will understand some of it. Then we can quietly pray in our hearts and say, "Thank You," to God for giving us teachers and pastors to tell us what He wants us to know. We can thank God for the church.

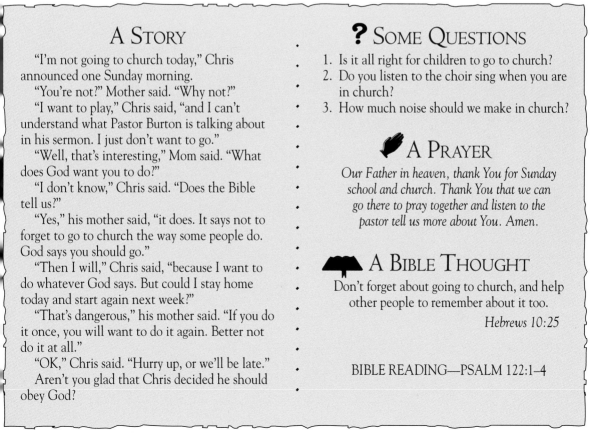

A STORY

"I'm not going to church today," Chris announced one Sunday morning.

"You're not?" Mother said. "Why not?"

"I want to play," Chris said, "and I can't understand what Pastor Burton is talking about in his sermon. I just don't want to go."

"Well, that's interesting," Mom said. "What does God want you to do?"

"I don't know," Chris said. "Does the Bible tell us?"

"Yes," his mother said, "it does. It says not to forget to go to church the way some people do. God says you should go."

"Then I will," Chris said, "because I want to do whatever God says. But could I stay home today and start again next week?"

"That's dangerous," his mother said. "If you do it once, you will want to do it again. Better not do it at all."

"OK," Chris said. "Hurry up, or we'll be late."

Aren't you glad that Chris decided he should obey God?

? SOME QUESTIONS

1. Is it all right for children to go to church?
2. Do you listen to the choir sing when you are in church?
3. How much noise should we make in church?

A PRAYER

Our Father in heaven, thank You for Sunday school and church. Thank You that we can go there to pray together and listen to the pastor tell us more about You. Amen.

A BIBLE THOUGHT

Don't forget about going to church, and help other people to remember about it too.

Hebrews 10:25

BIBLE READING—PSALM 122:1–4

It's not fun!

All of us are sick sometimes. When you are sick, sometimes you don't want to do anything except lie quietly in bed and sleep. Since the doctor has usually told your mother and father what is best for you, you should be careful to do just what they say. If you are supposed to stay in bed, then that is the best thing to do and not always be trying to get up. If you are supposed to eat only certain things, then don't beg for something else that might not be good for you to eat when you're sick.

There is something Christian boys or girls can do no matter whether they are well or sick. They can pray. Sometimes when you are sick you can do more for God than when you are well! You can pray for your friends and for missionaries far away. Perhaps that is the most important work that anyone can ever do.

And we can be happy and cheerful. That is important work too!

A Story

Linda was crying. "Oh, oh, oh!" she wailed. "My tummy hurts." Linda had been sick in bed all day, and she still felt bad all over.

"I'm sorry you aren't feeling well," Mom said, "but I think you'll feel better in the morning."

And, sure enough, when she woke up in the morning, and she felt much better.

"Can I get up and play?" she asked her mother. But Linda really wasn't quite sure she wanted to get up, because she still felt tired.

"No, not today," Mom said, "but maybe tomorrow."

"But, Mommy," Linda said, "I'll get too tired just being in bed all day."

"Oh," Mom said, "I think we can fix that. Let's think up some things to do."

Linda and Mom made a list. Linda told her mother what to write, and she wrote down what Linda said.

Here is the list:

Eat some breakfast   Pray for friends
Listen to the radio   Count cars going by
Sleep   Play with kitty
Play with dolls   Put together a jigsaw puzzle
Pray for Daddy at work

After Linda and her mother made the list, Linda felt tired and decided to take a nap. She slept all morning, and after lunch she did some of the things on her list, and before very long it was dinnertime. Linda's daddy came home with a new toy for her, so Linda had a nice day even though she was sick, and the next morning she could get up because she was all well again.

? Some Questions

1. Have you ever been sick? Did you find fun things to do?
2. Can you think of other things to do that Linda didn't put on her list?

✋ A Prayer

Lord, thank You for being with me when I am sick and when I am well. Help me to know always that You are near. I ask this in Jesus' name. Amen.

📖 A Bible Thought

When you are sick or in trouble
God will be right there with you.

Psalm 120:1

BIBLE READING—LUKE 18:35–43

Giving our money to Jesus

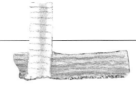

This big girl is holding a bankbook in her hands. The book tells how much money she has in the bank. She can go there and get her money whenever she wants it. The people at the bank will give her extra money, too, because she lets them use her money.

This girl's name is Suzanne, and whenever Suzanne gets any money, she gives part of it to God. She likes to take her money to Sunday school. She puts it in the offering at Sunday school. That's the way she gives it to God. So she takes some to Sunday school and takes some to the bank, and uses some to buy things she wants or needs.

All of our money, all of our clothes, and our houses belong to God. Everything we have belongs to Him. God lets us have these things to use, but they really belong to Him. Do you thank God for letting you use His things?

God will tell help you know what to do with His money. He will help you know how much to take to Sunday school, and how much to put in the bank, and how much to use to buy toys and clothes and other things. Whenever Suzanne gets $1.00 she takes 10¢ to Sunday School or church, to give to God.

A STORY

One day Suzanne—that is the name of this girl in the picture—made some cookies and took them to some other houses and asked the people in the other houses in her neighborhood, if they would like to buy some cookies. She said they could buy them for $3.00 a dozen. Many people wanted cookies, so Suzanne got $21.00. She gave some of the money to her mother to pay for the flour and sugar and butter she used to make the cookies. Then she put some in an envelope to give to missionaries. Then she went to the bank and gave some to the people there to keep for her. They marked her bankbook to tell how much money she had given to them to keep for her.

? SOME QUESTIONS

1. What is the girl's name?
2. What is she holding in her hand?
3. What did she do with the money she earned from selling cookies?

A PRAYER

Dear God in heaven, thank You for giving me so many good things to use. They are all Yours, but You let me use them, and I am glad. Help me to be careful with all Your things and use them as You want me to. Amen.

A BIBLE THOUGHT

It isn't good to want lots of money.

1 Timothy 6:10

BIBLE READING—MARK 10:23–27

Do you love God?

ow much do you love God? Do you love Him just a little bit, or do you love Him very much? If we love God a lot, we will do what He tells us to and then we will be happy. And then He will give us rewards and prizes for the good things we do.

But if we don't love God very much, then we won't even try to do what He wants us to. So you see, it makes a lot of difference whether you really love God or not. And God cares about it too. He wants you to love Him and if you don't, it makes Him sad.

Would you like to love God more? You can! All you need to do is to ask God to help you love Him more, and then He will send His Holy Spirit with so much love that you will have all you need.

Even a little child who has Jesus as His Savior may come to our heavenly Father and say, "Dear Father, I want to love You more and more. Please send the Holy Spirit to help me love You more." And God will gladly do this wonderful thing and help you love Him.

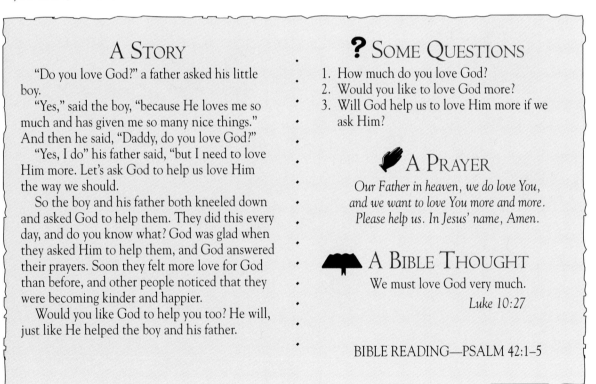

A Story

"Do you love God?" a father asked his little boy.

"Yes," said the boy, "because He loves me so much and has given me so many nice things." And then he said, "Daddy, do you love God?"

"Yes, I do" his father said, "but I need to love Him more. Let's ask God to help us love Him the way we should."

So the boy and his father both kneeled down and asked God to help them. They did this every day, and do you know what? God was glad when they asked Him to help them, and God answered their prayers. Soon they felt more love for God than before, and other people noticed that they were becoming kinder and happier.

Would you like God to help you too? He will, just like He helped the boy and his father.

? Some Questions

1. How much do you love God?
2. Would you like to love God more?
3. Will God help us to love Him more if we ask Him?

A Prayer

Our Father in heaven, we do love You, and we want to love You more and more. Please help us. In Jesus' name, Amen.

A Bible Thought

We must love God very much.
Luke 10:27

BIBLE READING—PSALM 42:1–5

Being a helper

This little girl is giving her puppy a bath. I wonder if the puppy is happy? Most puppies don't like to take baths, so maybe this one wants to jump out and run away.

But the puppy needs a bath, so it is good for the little girl to give him one. She's working hard getting him all clean and pretty. She is washing the puppy's ear.

The girl is being a good helper. Should I tell you why? It is because she likes to help and because she likes to do whatever she's asked to do. She knows it is right to help and not just do whatever she wants to. She knows that Jesus says to do whatever our mothers and fathers tell us to even when we don't want to.

This little girl can wash dishes and dry them, but she can't put them away easily because she can't reach up high enough. But she can put toys away and help keep the living room neat and clean.

Do you know any nice child at your house who can do all these things?

A STORY

Shannon and Jason weren't very happy at all. In fact, they were crying loudly. Just then Daddy walked into the room where they were.

"What a terrible noise," he said, "and what funny-looking faces. Whatever is the trouble?"

"Boo-hoo," cried Shannon and Jason. "Mommy asked us to help her put the knives and forks and spoons on the table. Boo-hoo, we don't want to."

"Why not?" Daddy asked. "We need them to eat dinner, don't we?"

"Yes," Shannon and Jason said, "but we shouldn't have to put them on."

"Who should then?" Daddy wanted to know.

Shannon and Jason stopped crying and looked at each other. They couldn't think of anybody else to do it. Mom was busy getting dinner ready, and Daddy had just come home.

"I guess we should," they said.

"Then you'd better do it." Daddy looked as if he didn't like the way they had been acting, so they ran into the kitchen and started to work fast!

? SOME QUESTIONS

1. What do you think would have happened to Jason and Shannon if they had just kept on crying instead of doing their work?
2. When you are asked to help do something, do you say, "Sure, I'll help," or do you complain and cry?
3. What does Jesus like us to do?

A PRAYER

Our Father, we need Your help to love other people as we should. Help us to love them and to help them. In Jesus' name we ask this. Amen.

A BIBLE THOUGHT

Be kind to each other.
Ephesians 4:31–32

BIBLE READING—EPHESIANS 6:1–4

The Lord's Table

Can you guess where these children are and what they are doing? They are in church, up near the front of the church, looking at the Communion table. On the table are plates full of little pieces of bread and little cups of grape juice. Have you seen a table like this in your church? Yes, I think you have. The food on the table is there because Jesus wants His friends to eat it.

Just before Jesus went away to die for us on the cross, He was eating with His friends. He told them to get together often and eat in this special way. God likes His children to do this. It is a time when we think about Jesus and His love. If we belong to Him, we remember that Jesus died for our sins and took them all away. When Christians eat this bread and drink the juice, they are doing what He told them to keep on doing until He comes again. So it is a time to be very glad that Jesus loves us and to be very sorry for bad things we have done.

How old should a child be before taking Communion? Different churches have different rules about this. But, first of all, children should love Jesus and know that He has died for their sins. Only people who love Jesus may eat this bread and drink from these cups.

A Story

Breanna was talking to her pastor. They were talking about Jesus and how much He loves children and their mothers and fathers. "Jesus died for me," Breanna said, "so He must love me very much."

"Yes, He was punished for what you did," her pastor said. "He died on the cross for your sins."

Then Breanna started to cry. "Yes," she said, "God hurt Jesus for what I did. Oh, I am so sorry for hurting Jesus, and I love Him so much. I want to do something to show Him how much I love Him." She thought about what she could do and decided to take some flowers to a neighbor who was sick.

? Some Questions

1. What did Breanna do to show Jesus that she loves Him?
2. What can you do?
3. When will you do it?

A Prayer

O God, our heavenly Father, how great You are! We cannot begin to tell You how thankful we are for Jesus and His great love. Thank You that Jesus came to die for me. Amen.

A Bible Thought

We love Him because He loved us first.

1 John 4:19

BIBLE READING—MATTHEW 26:26–29

Who is a guest?

These people in the picture are very happy because some friends have come to visit them. They haven't seen each other for a long time, and now they can enjoy being together again.

People who have come to visit are called "guests." Sometimes guests come just for dinner, and sometimes they stay all night and visit for several days.

It's fun when other kids come to visit. We can let them play with our toys. It's nice to help them have a good time.

Do you know that God likes us to have guests and invite people to eat with us? Yes, the Bible tells us. "Don't forget to invite people to come and visit."

Why does God like this? Because God loves for us to be friendly. He wants us to like other people and help them. And one way to make them happy is to ask them to come and visit us.

When guests are in your home, what are some ways to make them happy? One way is to help your mother. Perhaps you can help set the table or wash the dishes. It is interesting to talk to guests when Mommy and Daddy are busy. It's fun to find out things about where they live and interesting things they have seen and done.

A Story

Tami's mother was excited and happy, and Tami was too, because it was the day that Aunt Mae and Uncle George were coming for a visit. Aunt Mae and Uncle George didn't have any children for her to play with, but Tami was glad they were coming, because she knew they would talk and play with her. It was always fun when they came to visit.

As soon as their car drove up the driveway, Tami ran outside and gave Uncle George and Aunt Mae a great big kiss. By that time Mommy and Daddy were there too, and everyone was talking at the same time. So Tami went into the house and began to set the table for dinner. By the time Mommy and Daddy and Aunt Mae and Uncle George came in, her job was almost done.

Mommy said, "Oh, thank you, Tami. Now we can sit right down and eat. Thank you for setting the table so nicely."

Tami was happy because she had helped make Aunt Mae and Uncle George feel welcome.

? Some Questions

1. What did Tami do when she heard the car?
2. What did Tami do in the house?
3. Can you think of some guests you have had at your house? Who were they?
4. What are some ways to make guests happy?

A Prayer

Father, we thank You for letting us have friends to come and visit us. Help us to love them and to do kind things for them. Amen.

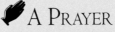 A Bible Thought

Don't forget to be kind to
people you don't know.

Hebrews 13:2

BIBLE READING—GENESIS 18:1–8

What is a missionary?

Who is this woman in the picture? She lives in a country far away. Her house looks different from yours, doesn't it? Can you see her little boy and little girl? The boy and his sister have never heard about Jesus. No one has ever told them that Jesus loves them. Would you like to go and tell them? If you do, you will be a missionary. A missionary is someone who goes and tells people about Jesus.

If you go to tell them about Jesus, you may not be able to talk to them at first, because these people don't talk like we do. They use different words. We say "good-bye" when someone is going away, but these people say "adios." All their words are different, so you will need to learn their words. Then you can talk to them about Jesus.

Do you know someone who is a missionary? Who is it? (Your mother or father can help you find out the name of a missionary you can pray for.)

Would you like to pray for children like this little girl and boy in the picture? Ask God to send someone to tell them about Jesus so they will know Him too, just as you do.

A Story

"I'm going to be a missionary when I get big," Tina told her mother. "I'm going to fly in an airplane and go far away and find somebody I can tell about Jesus."

"That's great," her mother said. "But you don't have to wait until you grow up to be a missionary. You can be a missionary now."

"Oh, good," Tina said. "Tomorrow is Sunday, so can I get in an airplane and go far away tomorrow and be a missionary?"

"No," her mother said, "but you can ride on your bike right now and go over to Mark Green's house and see if he can come to Sunday school with us tomorrow."

So Tina did. Mark said he would ask his mother if he could go to Sunday school with Tina, and his mother said yes.

Tina forgot about her bike and ran home as fast as she could. "Mama," she said, "Mark is going to go to Sunday school with me, so now am I a missionary?"

"Yes," her mother said, "you really are. You are a missionary to Mark now, and when you grow up you can be a missionary in some other country far away."

? Some Questions

1. Was Tina a missionary? Why?
2. Did Tina have to get into an airplane and go to another country to be a missionary?
3. Would you like to be a missionary? Can you think of someone to invite to Sunday school as Tina did?

 A Prayer

Our Father in heaven, help me to be a missionary and tell people about You. Help everybody to know that Jesus died for them. Amen.

A Bible Thought

Jesus said: Go everywhere and tell people about Me.

Mark 16:15

BIBLE READING—ISAIAH 52:7–10

It's good for families to pray together

Can you see what the people in this family are doing? Everyone has their eyes closed. They are praying. The father is talking out loud to God, and the mother and children are talking in their hearts so only God can hear them. Soon the mother will pray out loud, and each child will pray too.

After this family has talked to God, they will read from the Bible. Sometimes each one takes a turn reading a verse. Daddy and Mommy help the children who can't read. They say the words, and the children say them too.

Sometimes this family sings after they have read their Bible, and sometimes Daddy reads to them from a Bible storybook. Then they talk about things that have happened that day. sometimes they take turns and tell about things they are glad for or sorry about.

It is good for families to read the Bible together and to pray together and to talk together. God likes it when families do this.

A Story

Anne was visiting her friend Mary, who lived across the street. Mary's mother had asked her to stay for dinner so Anne was very happy. After the meal was over, Mary's father said, "Now it's time for family prayers."

"What are family prayers?" Anne wanted to know.

"Come and find out," Mary said, so the two little girls went into the living room with Mary's mother and father and two brothers, Jim and Kyle. First Mary's father read to them from a big book of Bible stories. He read about Jesus making a sick girl well again. Then they took turns praying. When it was Anne's turn, she said "Thank You, Jesus, for letting me come and listen to the Bible story."

After each one had prayed, they all sang, "Jesus loves me, this I know." Anne knew this song because she had learned it in Sunday school. That night, when Anne was home again and Daddy was tucking her into bed, she said, "Daddy, tomorrow let's have family prayers at our house too."

Her daddy thought that was a good idea, and now every night after dinner Anne and her mother and father and brothers and sister read the Bible and pray together. Isn't that a good idea?

? Some Questions

1. What did Anne tell her father when he was tucking her into bed?
2. How can a family pray?
3. Are family prayers good to have?

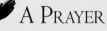 A Prayer

Dear Lord Jesus, thank You for loving all of us in our family. Thank You that we can pray together and read the Bible. Help us to understand it and to do what it says. In Your name. Amen.

A Bible Thought

If children learn to love the Lord at home, they will love Him all the rest of their lives.

Proverbs 22:6

BIBLE READING—DEUTERONOMY 6:6-9

The Bible is God's book

There is a song that children sometimes sing that goes like this:

> The B-I-B-L-E,
> Yes, that's the book for me
> I stand alone
> On the Word of God,
> The B-I-B-L-E.
> The B-I-B-L-E,
> Yes, that's the book for me.
> I read and pray
> And then obey
> The B-I-B-L-E.

Perhaps you know this song and have sung it many times in Sunday school. It's a good song because it talks about the Bible.

Do you have a Bible in your home? Yes, I am quite sure you do. But do you know who wrote the Bible? I want to tell you, because this is very important. God gave us the Bible by telling his friends what to write down. It is His Book. And God wants us to read His Book so we will know what He is telling us to do.

The Bible is like a letter. It is God's letter to you and to me. It doesn't look like a letter because it's so big, but it tells just what God wants us to know.

The Bible is a letter from God to you and me, and He wants us to read it.

A Story

"Mommy, did I get any letters from the mailman?" Cameron asked.

"There is a letter for you on the table," his mother said. "Why don't you read it now?"

"I don't see any letter," Cameron said. "Where is it? There is nothing on the table except my Bible."

"That's what I mean," his mother said. "That is your letter. It is a letter from God. Why don't you see what He says?"

"I guess I will," Cameron said. "I guess God wants me to read His letter. Will you help me read it?"

"Sure," his mother said. So Cameron and his mother sat down and read some of God's letter. Would you like to read God's letter too?

? Some Questions

1. Who wrote the Bible?
2. Does God want us to read His letter?
3. If you can't read, how can you find out what the Bible says?

A Prayer

Lord Jesus, thank You for telling us so many wonderful things in the Bible. Help us to understand them and to do whatever You want us to do. In Your name we ask these things. Amen.

A Bible Thought

God wrote everything that is in the Bible.

2 Timothy 3:16

BIBLE READING—NEHEMIAH 8:1–5

God's Invitation

Now we have come to the most important page in this book. It is the most important page because it tells us that Jesus died on the cross to keep God from punishing you and me for the wrong things we do. God loves us so much that He gave His only Son to die in our place. Jesus died for our sins so that we can be saved from God's anger and be given all of His love instead.

If you thank Jesus and tell Him you accept His offer to forgive your sins, He will welcome you forever into His family.

A Prayer

Oh God in heaven, thank you for sending Jesus to die for me. Now I accept Your offer of forgiveness and friendship. Amen.

A Bible Thought

God so loved the world that He gave His only son to die for you so that if you believe on His name you will have eternal life.

John 3:16